How Quetzalcoatl Brought
Chocolate
to the People

An Aztec Legend

Retold by Lynn Mesh

NATIONAL
GEOGRAPHIC
LEARNING

CENGAGE
Learning·

Long, long ago, the people on Earth did not have chocolate.

Back then, chocolate was a food that only the gods had. From the start of the world, the gods drank chocolate. They believed that chocolate made them wise and strong.

The gods didn't want the people to be wise or strong. The gods wanted to control the people. If the people were wise and strong, they would be difficult to control.

So the gods guarded the cacao tree, the tree from which chocolate is made, very closely. They kept the tree for themselves.

But one of the gods, Quetzalcoatl, did not want to keep chocolate from the people. Quetzalcoatl was a generous god. He taught the people how to farm, and he gave them corn. Without his help, the people on Earth would die.

The people were grateful to Quetzalcoatl. To show their thanks, they built temples to honor him.

Quetzalcoatl was pleased by this, so he decided to do something else for the people. He decided to share chocolate, the food of the gods, with them.

One spring day, Quetzalcoatl flew from the lands of the gods to Earth. He carried a cacao tree. The tree was covered with flowers.

Quetzalcoatl planted the tree and told the people how to take care of it. Then he returned to his home.

The people watered the tree and cared for it well.

That summer, the flowers disappeared, and large pods grew in their place. When the pods turned from green to a brown and red color, Quetzalcoatl returned. He pulled a pod from the tree and opened it. Inside, there were a handful of kernels.

Quetzalcoatl roasted the cacao kernels on a fire. A wonderful smell filled the air. Then he made a powder from the roasted kernels. That made the smell stronger and even more delicious.

Finally, Quetzalcoatl mixed the powder with hot water. He stirred the mixture so that it formed a paste. Then he added more water to make a thick liquid. He poured the liquid into golden cups and handed the hot chocolate out to the people. It was delicious!

Soon, everyone was drinking hot chocolate. The people smiled between sips.

From that day on, chocolate was everyone's favorite drink. The people grew many more cacao trees. They drank chocolate at celebrations, on holidays, and on every other special day.

Sometimes spices like cinnamon were added so the chocolate tasted even more delicious. Sometimes chilies were added so that the chocolate tasted spicy. Even when the drink was just chocolate and water, it always tasted good.

But the people liked chocolate for more than just its taste. Like the gods, the people believed that chocolate had special powers. Like the gods, when the people drank it, they felt wiser and stronger.

Soon the people, filled with chocolate, began to do amazing things. They created a system of math, and they learned about the stars. They created art and made music.

To thank Quetzalcoatl, they built big cities in his honor.

Quetzalcoatl was pleased.

But the other gods were not pleased.

They watched the people do great things, and they became angry.
They decided to punish Quetzalcoatl for sharing chocolate with the
people.

Tezcatlipoca, the god of night, was Quetzalcoatl's greatest enemy.
He planned to come to Earth disguised as an old woman to play a
terrible trick on Quetzalcoatl.

Just before Tezcatlipoca came to Earth, Quetzalcoatl had a bad
dream. In the dream, something terrible was about to happen. When
Quetzalcoatl woke up, he was very worried.

An old woman came over to Quetzalcoatl. (The old woman was really Tezcatlipoca.)

"What is wrong?" asked the old woman.

"I was sleeping, and I had a bad dream. The dream told me that something terrible is going to happen," Quetzalcoatl answered.

The old woman gave Quetzalcoatl a cup of blue liquid.

"Don't worry," she said. "Drink this. It will make you feel better. It will make you happy. It will make you wiser and stronger than ever."

"But this isn't chocolate," said Quetzalcoatl.

"It's better than chocolate!" said the woman.

Quetzalcoatl drank the liquid. Suddenly, his body felt as hot as fire. The liquid was a poison!

Quetzalcoatl began to run toward the ocean to cool his burning skin in the water.

As Quetzalcoatl ran, Tezcatlipoca burned all of the people's cacao trees.

When Quetzalcoatl reached the ocean, he stopped before he jumped in. He gave a chocolate pod to a man who was fishing there.

"Keep this," he said. "Use it to grow more chocolate trees when the time is right. Plant it and care for it like I showed you. Soon, the people will have chocolate again."

Quetzalcoatl disappeared into the ocean. The people never saw him again.

But the people still had his special gift. From that one chocolate pod, the people grew many cacao trees. Soon, cacao trees covered the land. Chocolate became more important to the people than gold!

This story of the origin of chocolate was told by the Aztec people. The ancient Aztecs lived long ago in the country that is now Mexico. The ancient Aztecs are gone now, but chocolate is still with us. Some say that chocolate is the Aztecs' special gift to the world.

Facts About Chocolate

Chocolate is the favorite treat of many people around the world. But how much do you know about chocolate? Here are some fun facts about this irresistible treat.

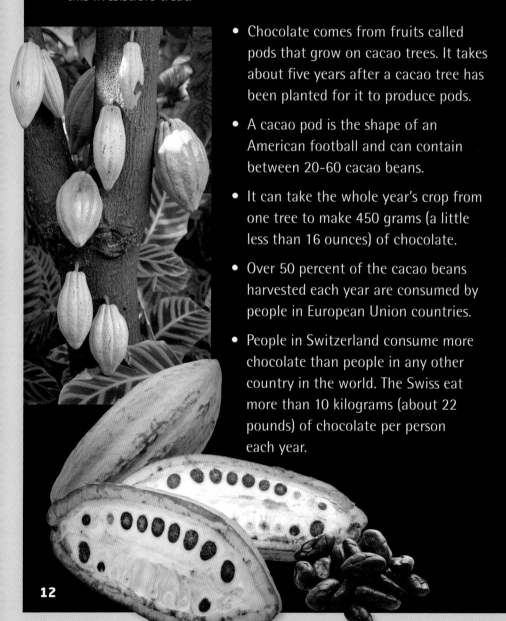

- Chocolate comes from fruits called pods that grow on cacao trees. It takes about five years after a cacao tree has been planted for it to produce pods.

- A cacao pod is the shape of an American football and can contain between 20-60 cacao beans.

- It can take the whole year's crop from one tree to make 450 grams (a little less than 16 ounces) of chocolate.

- Over 50 percent of the cacao beans harvested each year are consumed by people in European Union countries.

- People in Switzerland consume more chocolate than people in any other country in the world. The Swiss eat more than 10 kilograms (about 22 pounds) of chocolate per person each year.

- Africa produces about two-thirds of the world's cacao beans. But Africans don't consume much chocolate themselves. One reason is that chocolate becomes liquid at about 32°C (90°F), so it melts easily in countries with hot climates.

- Before 1847, there were no chocolate candy bars. Selling chocolate in a bar form was an idea created that year by a chocolate company in England.

- Chocolate can be good for you. There have been studies which show that eating chocolate, especially dark chocolate, may help keep your heart healthy.

- Chocolate contains chemicals that can make you feel happy!

Word Play Chocolate

Use the clues to fill in the crossword puzzle with the correct words.

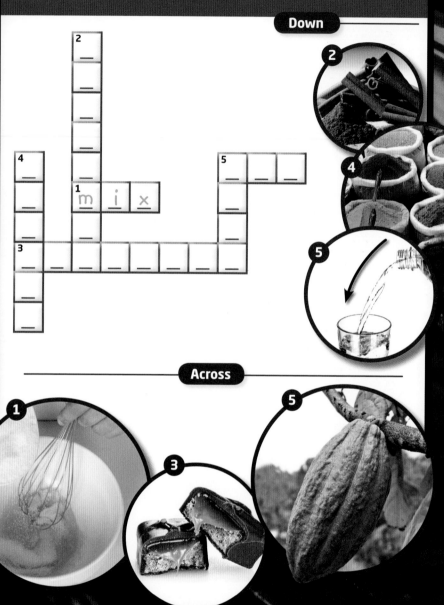

Down

2

4

5

Across

1

3

5

1 m i x

Look at the pictures. Write a short paragraph about them. Try to use as many of the words below as possible. Use a dictionary if necessary.

spices   hot chocolate   pod
candy bar   cinnamon   pour   mix

Glossary

chilies peppers with a hot, spicy taste

climate the type of weather that a place or region has

control to be in charge of something or someone

disappeared went completely out of sight

disguised changed what one looks like to trick someone

enemy a person who wants to hurt another person

generous kind and willing to give things to others

gods powerful beings who are not of this world and who are believed to have created humans and the human world

guarded protected

honor to show special respect for someone

irresistible not able to be refused

kernels seeds

poison a chemical or drug that can hurt or kill

roasted cooked

system an ordered, logical set of ideas

temples buildings built for worship of a god or gods

wise very smart